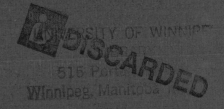

YES! CAPRA CHAPBOOK SERIES

number ten/yes! capra chapbook series

LOBA

part 1

❦

diane di prima

capra press   /   1973   /   santa barbara

Drawings by Josie Grant

Photo of Diane di Prima by Robert Durand

LOBA, PART 1 is from a work-in-progress.

ISBN 0-912264-69-1 (pa.)

ISBN 0-912264-70-5 (cl.)

CAPRA PRESS, 631 State Street, Santa Barbara, Ca. 93101

Other Books by Diane di Prima include:

THIS KIND OF BIRD FLIES BACKWARD
DINNERS AND NIGHTMARES
THE NEW HANDBOOK OF HEAVEN
MEMOIRS OF A BEATNIK
KERHONKSON JOURNAL
REVOLUTIONARY LETTERS
THE CALCULUS OF VARIATION.

O lost moon sisters
crescent in hair, sea underfoot do you wander
in blue veil, in green leaf, in tattered shawl do you wander
with goldleaf skin, with flaming hair do you wander
on Avenue A, on Bleecker Street do you wander
on Rampart Street, on Fillmore Street do you wander
with flower wreath, with jeweled breath do you wander

      footprints
                shining mother of pearl
                        behind you
      moonstone eyes
                in which the crescent moon

with gloves, with hat, in rags, in fur, in beads
under the waning moon, hair streaming in black rain
wailing with stray dogs, hissing in doorways
shadows you are, that fall on the crossroads, highways

jaywalking do you wander
spitting do you wander
mumbling and crying do you wander
aged and talking to yourselves

9)

with roving eyes do you wander
hot for quick love do you wander
weeping your dead

    naked you walk
    swathed in long robes you walk
    swaddled in death shroud you walk
    backwards you walk

        hungry
        hungry
        hungry

    shrieking I hear you
    singing I hear you
    cursing I hear you
    praying I hear you

        you lie with the unicorn
        you lie with the cobra
        you lie in the dry grass
        you lie with the yetti
        you flick long cocks of satyrs with your tongue

10)

                    you are armed
                    you drive chariots
                    you tower above me
                    you are small
                    you cower on hillsides
                    out of the winds

pregnant you wander
barefoot you wander
battered by drunk men you wander

                    you kill on steel tables
                    you birth in black beds
                            fetus you tore out stiffens in snow
                            it rises like new moon
                            you moan in your sleep

digging for yams you wander
looking for dope you wander
playing with birds you wander
chipping at stone you wander

11)

I walk the long night seeking you
I climb the sea crest seeking you
I lie on the prairie, batter at stone gates
calling your names

you are coral
you are lapis and turquoise
your brain curls like shell
you dance on hills

hard-substance-woman you whirl
you dance on subways
you sprawl in tenements
children lick at your tits

you are the hills, the shape and color of mesa
you are the tent, the lodge of skins, the hogan
the buffalo robes, the quilt, the knitted afghan
you are the cauldron and the evening star
you rise over the sea, you ride the dark

I move within you, light the evening fire
I dip my hand in you and eat your flesh

12)

you are my mirror image and my sister
you disappear like smoke on misty hills
you lead me through dream forest on horseback
large gypsy mother, I lean my head on your back

I am you
and I must become you
I have been you
and I must become you
I am always you
I must become you

ay-a
ay-a ah
ay-a
ay-a ah ah
maya ma maya ma
om star mother ma om
maya ma ah

DECEMBER 1971

13)

LOBA
part 1

"It would be very pleasant to die with a wolf woman
It would be very pleasant"

— Tlingit Song

"A clever man builds a city
A clever woman lays one low"

— Shi Ching

I.

if he did not come apart in her hands, he fell
like flint on her ribs, there was no
middle way, the rocks screamed
in the flowing water; stars dizzy
w/pain, if he was not
daisies in her soup he was another
nettle in her hair, she stumbled
crazy over the stony path between
slanderous trees; even field mice knew
she called the shots, dimensions
of the obsidian cross he
hung on, singing in the sun, her eyes
cloudy w/nightmare, she grinned
baring her wolf's teeth. . . .

Who will describe the triumph streaming
out of her pelt, the symphonies
wind carried to her fine nose?
Her walk, graceful but never feline
shoulders moving as she strode
through undergrowth, dew from the ferns
wet her tits, her short, clear barks?

18)

And if she bends, eternally, at tables
at wood tables in factories, fashioning
crosses of silver, this time, inlaid
with jet & abalone, will you meet
her eyes, she
raises her head. . . .

19)

Is she city? Gate she is we know
& has been, but the road
paved w/white stones? her paws
are cut by it, the lights
blind her, yet she knows, she comes
to it, white porcelain lining
dome of her brain, she flies
to it on broomstick, on gold mandala
platter or calendar, she sits, her tail
curled round her neat white paws. . . .

20)

Signals. Does she stream, in
wind, her nose riding channels
of the seven rays, the planets
vibrating in her brain, the curling
canals of her guts? Strait as
her eyes, her spine
cd be, but it curves, she curves it
around weeds, she lies down
in the sun.

See how her tit drags on the ground.
She steps on it. She *baaa*'s
She keens, as an old black goat, waiting
blow of the ax. Feel head roll on
wet earth, blood spout (fountain)
from neck, strong as column.
See her dance.

See the young, black, naked woman riding
a dead white man. Her hair
greasy, she whips him & he flies
thru the smoky air. Her hand
is in her mouth, she is eating
flesh, it stinks, snakes wind
around her ankles. Her hand
touches the (wet) earth. Her hand
shakes a gourd rattle, she laughs, her fangs
flash white & red, they are set
with rubies.

see how old woman's tits hang down
on that young, lithe body, know the skull
in her hand your own, she eats
your eyes & then your brain. . . .

Hush, the old-young woman
touches you, she is gold, she wears
a peaked cap, vines
grow out of it. Her tongue flicks
at the corners of her mouth. She says
        "The white gold
          almost invisible is made
          from the red-yellow metal, it is
          the Link." Bodies
pass out of hers, doubles
in silver, copper, iron. Glistening. They lick
their lips. They float on out. Her eyes
show waters parting a jungle, her arms
are vines around you, her tongue
is growing in your mouth. She
thrusts a finger deep into your cunt.

25)

If you do not come apart like bread
in her hands, she falls
like steel on your heart. The flesh
knows better than the spirit what the soul
has eyes for. Has she sunk
root in yr watering place, does she look
w/her wolf's eyes out of your head?

SKETCHES OF THE LOBA

She stood in the dark bar trying
to turn him into a cobra.
To grow those three horns into
the old, familiar hood.

*   *   *   *   *   *

O the soft
red walls she clung to, they held
her only for a second, she came down
in a torrent of blood

*   *   *   *   *   *

It is snowing in the jungle of her pelt,
                    the crystals
Dance in her cavernous nostrils.

How he drew her down to pleasure! She left
the flickering ice for the candlelight to watch
him bending his head w/the weight
of invisible antlers. It was a role
she was tired of playing. In her
mind's eye she saw herself loping across Europe
naked & lean on the beaches, presiding
at gypsy festivals. She glimmered
black & white like some elusive

                    opal. Who wd
brush donkey shit off her skirt, lick
the beach tar off her feet by the flickering
grey seas of the north? In the candlelight she moved
                    her hands, her rings
played, she moved, her face, her mouth, her voice
fell like water on him.

THE LOBA DANCES

She raises
      in flames
           the

city
   it glows about her
          The Loba

mother wolf &
       mistress

of many
     dances she

treads
    in the severed heads
           that grow

like mosses
      on the flood
         the city

melts it
    flows past her

treading
   white feet they

29)

curl around
            ashes & the ashes
sing, they chant
                a new
                    creation myth
ghoul lips of
            lovers she
                        left
like pearls
            in the road
                        she
dances, see

her eyes
        glow the
                city
glows dancing
            in them
                    wolf cry you hear
falls
    from the stars
                the Loba

30)

dances, she
               treads the
salty earth, she
                  does not
                         raise
breath cloud heavenward
                       her breath
itself
    is carnage.

This chapbook series, edited by Robert Durand (Yes! Press) and Noel Young (Capra Press), is designed and printed by Capra Press in Santa Barbara. This is the tenth title in the series, published May 1973. One hundred numbered copies, signed by the poet, were handbound.